Healthy & Homemade: Eating Well on a Budget

By JuJu Harris

DEDICATED TO MY DEAR FAMILY

Valentin, Zendeki, and Zazu, and to my Southern DC Chapter

Mocha Moms who allowed me to share food with them and

helped me find my niche.

ACKNOWLEDGMENTS

Cover Photo by: Eugene Buonaccorsi

Graphic Design: Elizabeth Samolis

Forward by: Monica Utsey

CONTENTS

FOREWORD: MEETING NANA JUJU

I remember the first time I saw her. I assumed she was a well-to-do woman who was married to a white man, since her son Zen is so fair skinned. I was sitting across from her at a breast-feeding peer counseling meeting. We are warrior mamas committed to breastfeeding and we wanted to help other mothers do the same.

As we took turns introducing ourselves, I had already formed an opinion about her. I could not have been more wrong! JuJu introduced herself in a transparent way, sharing that she was married to a Paraguayan campesino cotton farmer, lived with her mother and was also a WIC (Women Infant and Children nutrition program) recipient. Wow! This woman is bold, I thought to myself. My next thought was how wrong I was to make assumptions. I was intrigued that despite her own personal circumstances, she wanted to help others.

At the time, I was the new founder and President of the Southern DC Chapter of Mocha Moms. I had broken away from the original DC Chapter, because I wanted to create a place for us crunchy-granola, breastfeeding, baby wearing, co-sleeping mamas. Part of the mission of the Southern DC Chapter of Mocha Moms was to provide support to new mothers. During our weekly support group meetings, we talked about everything related to marriage and family. One of the re-occurring conversations was "what to cook for dinner?" Many of us could not cook and quite frankly, didn't want to. Nana JuJu came to the rescue. We made "Cook Day with Nana JuJu" a part of our chapter's monthly programming. Cook Day gave us the opportunity to cook together, to laugh, to learn, just like our sisters on the continent. We would arrive early in the day with our ingredients, ready to laugh and learn.

1

On the second Cook Day, JuJu had us make lemon mousse, focaccia, and roasted veggies. Our friend walked in with a spotless roasting pan and beater, and JuJu said, "you take really good care of your utensils." She replied, "oh, these are brand new. I almost didn't come because I didn't have either of these, but my husband said if it meant that I'd learn to cook, he'd buy me whatever I needed. So, he ran right out to Target." I didn't measure out the yeast for my bread, and our friend threw her butter into a mixing bowl. JuJu said "Honey, that's not a saucepan. You can't put that on the stove. So, ladies, let's start simply. Let's go over the recipes first and see that you have everything." She rolled her eyes and said, laughing, I should have had you start with lemonade first!" I'd brought canned tomatoes for the roasted veg, and my husband, Eric fussed and said "look, next time JuJu sends you a shopping list, send it to me so I can get the right stuff." At one point I said "Whew! Do you cook like this every day?" JuJu replied, "yes, but it doesn't take me five hours to get through a recipe!"

That Cook Day, there were 22 kids, 15 moms, and my husband. (He claims that he didn't want to get stuck in traffic. I said "what traffic?! It's 11am!") Only two of us were cooking, our friend's 6-year-old son, "The Professor" was leading the kids in the garden, turning over every rock gathering bugs. One sister was holding court talking about her organizational techniques. Zazu, JuJu's infant son, was somewhere in the mix, in someone's arms, being loved up, in her home that embraced us all. It felt like a family reunion, wonderful!!

On Cook Days, I learned how to chop, dice, and slice while laughing about potty-training, laundry, finances or whatever the hot topic was of the day. It was a beautiful time in space in the middle of the day when our spouses were at work. By the time the day was done, we all left with a full cooked meal and our spouses never knew how much fun we had. For all they knew, we had been standing over a hot stove all day. Our husbands even started asking "when is JuJu having another Cook Day?" because they were so pleased with the new dishes that we brought home.

I learned so much during those Cook Days. I learned about the beauty of cooking and the importance of the person who prepares the food. The family cook is also the family nutritionist and has the power to heal. I have so many pleasant memories from those days, from our children frolicking in the yard, naked running through the water sprinklers while we watched out of the window, to the first cheese quesadilla I made. Nana JuJu's Cook Day probably saved some marriages. She showed us that when you cook from love, the food is so much better.

Monica Utsey is a journalist, homeschooler and founding member of the Southern DC Mocha Moms chapter.

MY CULINARY STORY

Once upon a time I couldn't cook anything other than steak and an iceberg lettuce salad with bottled Ranch dressing. One day my sister and I made dinner for our dad. I made chili, she made vanilla cake with super sweet pink icing. Afterwards, she and I had a fist fight over what had made Daddy puke, the cake, or the chili.

I grew up in East Oakland, California. My dad worked for the government and my mom was, in turn, a homemaker, a 4-H leader, a parent-child educator. My mom loathed cooking, as she was one of the oldest in a family of 8 kids and had been cooking ever since she could remember. Even so, she dutifully had dinner on the table each night when my dad came home, and we'd eat together every night. I cringe, now, thinking about her food. Leftover (dried out) roast beef was thinly sliced, mixed with cans of Chun King bean sprouts and water chestnuts, a large splash of soy sauce, and served with mushy white rice, as "Chinese Food." Neon orange ambrosia, composed of cottage cheese, orange Jell-O, tangerines and coconut was dessert. And oh my!! Her stuffing was so dry! I once cautioned a Thanksgiving guest to have a glass of liquid at hand in case he started to choke on it.

My passion for the connection between health and food was sparked when I saw my father successfully manage high blood pressure, high cholesterol, obesity, and borderline diabetes through diet and exercise. I really hit my cooking stride when my first husband told me that no-one could ever cook as well as his gramma could. I took it as my personal mission to beat her. I remember going to the store, and carefully shopping for ingredients to make a minestrone soup. At the time, I didn't work for 6 months, and every day when he came home, a delicious home cooked meal would be waiting for him. I knew I'd "won" when he declared that my food beat his Nonna's.

I married my Paraguayan sweetheart, whom I'd met when I was a Peace Corps Agriculture Volunteer there in 1996. Valentin was a subsistence farmer, growing cotton, and tobacco for his main cash crops. His farm backed onto my host family's, and he would come over to help with chores. One day, he came over to capture a wild beehive, so I sat down with my host sister to watch. He took off his long, raggedy pants, worn over shorts, climbed the tree and chopped down the branch, capturing the colony. When I tell the story now, I say "He put a machete between his teeth, climbed up the trunk, and I thought 'oh, you Tarzan, me Jane!" My sister asked in Guarani, the indigenous language "Don't you think he's handsome?" "He's not too ugly", I said. "Don't you want him for your boyfriend?" I knew that Valentin had kids, so I replied in my lousy Guarani, meaning to say that he is already married, "Omonoma" (He's dead already). She bellowed with laughter, telling me the correct word. "Dead. Married. It's the same thing, depending on who you're married to," I quipped.

My job as an Agriculture Volunteer was to teach the men better farming techniques to reduce erosion, and to introduce new crops. However, I naturally spent more time with the women, and observed their daily challenge of raising children, often without a husband. I was particularly close to Valentin's family, as his ex-wife was kind and encouraged me to visit her and their children. The children showed signs of malnutrition and had skin worms, and when I asked why she didn't purchase medicine, she laughed bitterly, and said "I don't have any money, Julia." I asked Valentin the same thing, and he replied likewise. I saw their shame that they were unable to care for their children, and almost a resignation that their poverty would make it so forever.

I started paying more attention to the women lives, and how they managed with little income. What did they prioritize for purchase? What necessary items did their kids lack? How did they manage if there was an emergency? Then, I wondered "How do women and their families in the United States deal with poverty?"

I had to leave Peace Corps service early, ordered to leave the village for my safety. By then, Vale and I had been dating for a few months. I returned home to Oakland, California. In need of closure, I returned to Paraguay 7 months later to see him face to face. We ended up living in a slab board house that he'd built, with a dirt floor, no electricity, and a literal hole for a toilet.

I grew up on what I call the "Disney Lie", you know, the one they sell little girls... that one day a prince will come, marry you and take you away to a life of ease and wealth. Well, when I married Valentin, he had pretty much nothing. We lived with my mom the first two years here in Maryland. I had a high-risk pregnancy, so I didn't work. Money was crazy tight, and I was so stressed out. However, I was determined to "grow" the healthiest baby possible, so I used staples purchased with my WIC checks to make healthy, nutrient dense meals. I breastfed Zen for 3 years and I know that breastfeeding and my diet are the reasons that he rarely got sick.

When I was pregnant with Zazu, I joined the Southern DC Chapter of the Mocha Moms. I met a couple of moms who said, "I cook the same old stuff, even though I know it's not good for me." They didn't know what different ingredients looked or tasted like and were afraid to experiment because if the meal bombed, they would have wasted money and food. I thought "if you can read and follow directions, you can cook." But I realized that it's not that simple. A lot of teaching and learning goes on from spending time in the kitchen and cooking with someone.

You can't learn how bread dough should feel from watching a cooking show. You can't learn how "toasted" spice such as cumin seed or coriander seed should smell until you stir it around in a skillet. And how are you supposed to know if a vegetable or fruit is a "good" one, if no-one has ever taken you shopping to show you?

I held Cook Days at my home and taught my Mocha Mom friends how to make new dishes while our kids played outside. I'd send a recipe, a list of ingredients and cooking utensils needed. I assured them that in the time it takes to listen to a Stevie Wonder album, it's possible to have dinner cooked and on the table. One mom commented that her husband couldn't taste the love in her food. Yes, I agreed that it can be tedious chopping and stirring, stressful even figuring out what to cook in the first place. For me, it's not so much the spices or ingredients you use in your food that makes it good; it's the attitude and energy that surrounds the preparation of the meal, the setting of the table, the feelings that breaking bread with a loved one generates.

For meal planning, I figure out the basic ingredients to have on hand, things that I always cook with and keep my cupboards stocked with those things, such as potatoes, onions, carrots, cilantro. Then I read all sorts of cookbooks... Korean, Lebanese, vegan, Latino, foods from the Motherland and all the African Diaspora. I consider what I know the rest of the family will eat (noodles, rice), but since I'm more adventurous with trying new foods, I choose what appeals to me. Therefore, I add the specific ingredients called for in the recipe to my grocery list, for example, black mustard seed, red lentils, and coconut milk. Then I cook the food and put it on the table. Of course, others can make requests, so from time to time I'll make what they ask for.

My advice is to be more adventurous in your own choices and explore food together. If you find cooking tedious or stressful, try this. Take a food that's familiar, like grilled cheese sandwiches, and look for another cultures' version of that... a Mexican quesadilla (cheese on a tortilla) or an El Salvadorian pupusa (cheese or beans inside grilled corn dough). If you can make chicken or beef stew, you can plop some dough on top of it and make it pot pie or put mashed potatoes on top for Shepherd's pie. Replace the meat with vegetables for another version of each of those. For a spin on meatballs, try ground turkey and make Indian meatballs. My kids were surprised that they were eating meat that had cinnamon and freshly grated ginger as two of the ingredients. I made a Vietnamese beef stew that had star anise and beer in it. My dinner pot is like a box of chocolates. You never know what you're going to get.

I keep lunches simple. Often, it's quesadillas, a quick veggie soup with noodles, and fruit. Sometimes they eat fried eggs. When I cook beans, I make extra to freeze for later and we'll eat that with corn tortillas, cheese, and guacamole. It's expensive to take my kids out to lunch, and I will not buy them fast food, so I'll cook oven-fried chicken and bring fruit and water for them if we're going on an outing.

At one point, there were nine of us in this household, composed of the blended families of our sons, Valentin's kids, and my nephew. I was still receiving WIC and only Vale was working. My new kids were malnourished, and we were vegetarians at the time to non-medically manage Vale's cholesterol. The kids refused to eat what I cooked, and I was advised to feed them whatever they wanted to eat, to get "good fat on them," and then switch back to our regular diet. They loaded up on fried eggs and hot dogs, quesadillas, fried ham, and meat soup. I still cooked vegetarian dishes, and eventually they grew accustomed to my cooking.

In 2009, Valentin was in a motorcycle accident, which required an 18-month rehabilitation. I was offered a job teaching gardening, nutrition, and cooking to children in an afterschool program. Our food budget for our then, family of 4 was $100 cash and a huge vegetable and herb garden, supplemented by $219 from SNAP (Supplemental Nutrition Assistance Program/aka Food Stamps; 2021 value $271) benefits. With such a limited budget, I had to be very creative. I planned primarily meatless meals, based on vegetables that were inexpensive and used fresh herbs to augment flavor.

One day I said "I wish I knew something about politics or education. Then I could do something positive in the community." My girlfriends said "JuJu, you know food! You know how to teach people to make a feast using simple ingredients." I started doing cooking demonstrations at Farmers' Markets in DC, spreading what I call my "gospel of eating well." My philosophy, my "good news," is that healthy eating need not be expensive, difficult or time consuming.

I parlayed my experience as a former WIC and SNAP recipient and my culinary knowledge into a successful profession, authoring a cookbook, teaching children and adults in the community at Farmers' Markets, after-school programs, and senior centers. Most recently, I worked as the Culinary Educator on a mobile farmers' market, which served areas in DC which lacked a sufficient number of full-service grocery stores. I left that position to pursue studies as a birth and post-partum doula, and plan ultimately to combine my love of teaching about healthy cooking with my love of moms and babies.

I usually make a grocery list before I head to the store and check my pantry staples. I don't go hungry, to avoid spur of the moment purchases, and I carried snacks with me for my boys when they were small.

When I am meal planning, I take several points into account, asking:

- Is it healthy?

- Is it delicious?

- Is it budget friendly?

- Is it flexible? How else can I cook this?

- Can I substitute an ingredient if there is something on sale?

Many of the recipes in this cookbook are based on WIC staples, developed when I received it when my boys were little. Other recipes were created in the ensuing years to feed my tribe of nine, or to accommodate the quantities of food that my now growing teen boys and hardworking husband need to thrive.

Some sample dishes inspired during this time:

PANTRY STAPLES: potatoes, carrots, onions, ginger, garlic, butternut squash, greens (Swiss Chard, Spinach, Kale), craisins, rolled oats, flour, honey, nuts, oil, chicken, sausage, ground turkey

POTATOES:

Spanish Potato Torte with Stir Fried Greens

Roasted Chicken with Potatoes, Carrots, Onions
(which can be transformed into soup and chicken salad sandwiches next day)

Home Fries and Onions with Sausage and Carrot Juice
(Breakfast for Dinner)

CARROTS:

Carrot Ginger Soup with Oatmeal Bread and Salad

Roasted Vegetables with Garbanzo Beans over Rice
(Add vinaigrette for a salad lunch for the next day)

Sausage with Honeyed Carrots, Mashed Potatoes and Steamed Greens

GROUND TURKEY

Turkey Soup with Meatballs

Chicken and Meatball Casserole
(Add potatoes, carrots, onions, garlic, and greens)

Turkey Burgers with Lemon Bean Salad and Ginger Iced Tea

RESOURCES FOR EATING ON A BUDGET

GROW YOUR OWN: One of my first memories is of my mother... A cigarette clenched in her teeth, spraying her shrubs with chemicals to kill aphids, while my sister and I sat playing nearby. At that time, the effect of pesticides (and cigarette smoke!) on children's health wasn't widely known, so my mom didn't know that she was doing anything wrong. Years later, as the benefits of organic food were more widely touted, I taught myself to garden, eschewing the use of chemicals on my homegrown food. I use only leaf mulch, aged kitchen compost and manure, and fish emulsion on my vegetables. Every year, I save my new seed catalogs to read on the first stormy day and sit by the fire happily circling descriptions that look interesting. Then the reality of the year's seed budget pops into my head, and I go back and revise my list.

There are a plethora of books and online resources on gardening. In addition, state Agricultural Extension Agencies offer Master Gardener classes, and local parks and recreation departments may offer free or low-cost gardening classes. An amazing amount of food can be grown in containers by apartment dwellers. If you don't have a yard or balcony, you can post a notice to see if anyone is willing to let you garden in their yard in exchange for produce.

FARMERS' MARKETS: Strolling through a Farmers' Market is one of my favorite past times. I love to walk the entire market, checking to see whose produce is freshest and at the best price. Sometimes there is a local musician performing, often there are samples of products or a cooking demonstration. After several visits, I get to know the vendors by name, and they get to know me. Farming is such hard work, that I never haggle on prices and handle their fruit with care as I make my choices, to avoid bruising. Some farmers will sell their "seconds" at a reduced price, or even give them away at the end of the market day to avoid having to haul it back to the farm. Damaged or "ugly" produce is just as useful as the more "perfect" pieces, and can be used for jams, stocks, or sauces.

Eating local is an all-around benefit for all. The farmer wins because they can sell their produce within a day or even hours of its harvest, and they receive a fair price for their labor. The customer receives food that is more nutrient intact than that which has been harvested before it is optimally ripening time, and then trucked or shipped miles to the store before it is consumed. The environment benefits because less pollution is created from transporting products a shorter distance.

Beautiful food sold at a fair price from the farmer to the consumer moved over shorter distances equals a healthier, more economically viable system for the community.

COMMUNITY SUPPORTED AGRICULTURE: Community Supported Agriculture (CSA) is an amazing option for obtaining recently harvested, fresh produce and saving money. Farmers sell shares at the beginning of the planting season, and customers receive fresh produce each week from the growing season. In addition, farms offer you-pick options, so that customers can harvest additional produce and/or flowers. Many farms accept SNAP as well, charging benefits weekly instead of collecting the total amount at the beginning of the year. Some CSAs offer workshares, where food can be earned in exchange for help harvesting, washing, or sorting food on the farm. Food can be picked up on the farm or at a local farmers' market, or in some cases, delivered. You'll get to know your farmer and support a local business.

LOCAL STOCKYARDS AND HUNTING: A friend asked Valentin "What do you miss most about Paraguay?" My man replied, "I miss fresh meat." He was raised on a cattle ranch, where animals were slaughtered for meat, as needed. Most meat in the United States is produced on a large scale, with antibiotics used to manage disease common in crowded, stressful conditions. The meat in the store has the "use by date", but not the date of the animal's death. How old is this, I wonder? What was it raised on? I want to eat as little "factory farmed" food as possible to reduce our antibiotic intake, and store-bought organic meat is out of our budget. Therefore, we do what I call a "Kill and Grill."

Being raised on a cattle ranch, Valentin is handy with a knife. There are small livestock farms nearby where he purchases goats, pigs or sheep and brings them home to butcher in the backyard. For about $150, we get 40-50 pounds of meat, plus blood for sausage, the bones for stock and the skin for rugs or crafts. In the Fall, we receive deer as gifts, and have 100 pounds of venison for stews, sausage, and jerky. I was pretty grossed out by the slaughter and would leave the house but realized that if I was going to eat meat, then I should be present when the animal died. If the thought of slaughtering makes you queasy, some stockyards will slaughter the animal for you for a nominal fee.

FOOD RECLAMATION (AKA DUMPSTER DIVING AND GLEANING): Half of the food grown in fields never makes it to grocery stores, because it didn't meet size or quality standards for market. Much of the food in grocery stores is discarded because it is bruised, nearing its "sell by" date or the packaging has been compromised. However, it is still edible!

I've met folks who have no qualms about literally climbing into dumpsters to retrieve food. I don't do that since I'm afraid of getting cut on a rusty can or poked by a nail. Some stores are willing to directly donate food removed from display.

For example, my friend supplements several families' food stock with items picked up once a week from a national grocery chain. Variety depends, of course, on what has been culled, but I've gotten mounds of organic fruit, coffee, dog food, cheese, and baked goods. Once there was even pasture raised meat since the store's freezers had malfunctioned overnight. I've made dozens of jars of tomato jam, peach jelly, roasted bell peppers, and applesauce from food I've acquired this way.

Store discards even include bouquets of flowers with which I have used to decorate my home. Bakeries usually have a mountain of bread, their "over-bake", that is tossed in the garbage. I've made croutons and breadcrumbs from loaves left on the loading dock.

Some farmers allow groups to go through their fields to gather what has been left after the main harvest. Contact your local regional gleaning network for information.

PANTRY STAPLES

Spices *(fresh or dried)*:

Sea salt

Black pepper

Ground cumin

Crushed red pepper

Garlic

Basil

Oregano

Parsley

Bay leaves

Onion powder

Chili powder

Ground cinnamon

Ginger *(Fresh or Ground)*

Vanilla extract

Refrigerator:

Butter, Milk, Eggs

Greek yogurt

Frozen vegetables

Baking:

Sugar or sweetener

Unbleached flour

Yeast

(refrigerate after opening)

Baking Soda and

Baking Powder

Condiments:

Olive oil *(for salad dressing)*

Vegetable oil *(for frying)*

Vinegar

(rice, apple, cider, balsamic)

Mustard

Ketchup

Barbecue sauce

Salsa

Soy sauce

Hot sauce

Honey

Mayonnaise

Dry Foods:

Beans *(lentils, black, garbanzo, pinto)*

Nut Butter

Canned Tomatoes

Pasta

Rice *(brown, basmati, jasmine)*

Canned fruit in juice

Canned vegetables

Old-Fashioned (rolled) or Irish Oats

Onions, Potatoes, Carrots

Winter Squash

COOK'S TOOLS

Baking Sheets: Choose heavy-duty metal sheets with raised edges.

Blender: For making salad dressings, soups, smoothies, sauces, and pastes.

Cake Pans: The most common sizes are 8- or 9-inch rounds with 1 1/2 -2-inch sides.

Colander: Great for rinsing vegetables, small fruit or draining pasta.

Dutch Oven (Casserole): A large, heavy pot with a tight-fitting lid used for slow cooking on the stove or in the oven. Can also be used to bake bread.

Garlic Press: Minces garlic quickly.

Grater: Used to grate cheese, lemon or orange peel into salad dressings or cakes. Box graters stand on their own and have multiple size holes.

Knife, Chef's: Usually 8 to 10-inches, this is a heavy, long knife with a wide blade at the base that gently curves and comes to a point. Used for chopping, slicing, and dicing.

Knife, Paring: A sharp and maneuverable, 4-inch version of the chef's knife. Used for de-stemming, paring, and slicing small fruits, and doing other tasks that a large knife would overwhelm.

Ladle: Choose one with a heat-resistant handle and that is large enough to scoop up good-sized portions of soups and stews.

Loaf Pans: Can be metal or glass and come in a standard size of 9x5x3 inches, used to bake bread or desserts.

Measuring Cups, Dry: Made of plastic or metal and bundled as a set, in graduated sizes.

Measuring Cups, Liquid: Usually glass or plastic, the best liquid measures are sold in 1-, 2-, and 4-cup sizes.

Measuring Spoons: A spoon set that generally ranges from 1/8 teaspoon to 1 Tablespoon.

Metal Spatula: For flipping pancakes, burgers, or stir-frying.

Mixing Bowls: Stainless steel is the best choice because plastic bowls may absorb smells.

Muffin/Cupcake Pan: For sweets, bread, cornbread, breakfast, or mini quiches.

Potato Peeler: Removes the skin from root vegetables or makes thin slices of vegetables.

Rubber Spatula: Used to scrape batter or sauces from bowls and jars.

Sauce Pans: Stainless steel lasts the longest. Avoid aluminum pans, whose thinness allows food to scorch easily.

Skillets (Frying Pans): Sloped, shallow pans let food brown better. Look for ones with oven-proof metal handles, which can go straight in the oven. Plastic handles will melt.

Stock Pot: A tall, deep, large-capacity pot (10-12 quarts is a useful size) with a tightly fitting lid. Used for making stocks, soups, or boiling pasta.

Strainer (Sieve): Separates large particles from smaller, pasta from water, and can also be used for sifting flour.

Whisk: For beating eggs, making salad dressings, and making batter.

Wooden Spoons: Used for mixing dough, stirring soup, or tossing salads.

COMMON COOKING TERMS

<u>Bake:</u> To cook food, covered or uncovered, using the direct, dry heat of an oven. The term usually describes the cooking of cakes, cookies, casseroles, and breads.

<u>Braise:</u> To cook food slowly in a small amount of liquid in a tightly covered pan on the range top or in the oven. Braising is recommended for less-tender cuts of meat. Long, slow cooking makes the meat tender.

<u>Beat:</u> To make a mixture smooth by briskly whipping or stirring with a spoon, fork, whisk beater, or electric mixer.

<u>Blend:</u> To combine two or more ingredients by hand, or with an electric mixer/blender, until smooth and uniform in texture, flavor, and color.

<u>Cream:</u> To beat two ingredients with a wooden spoon and a bit of elbow grease or an electric mixer until they form a light, uniform, and creamy mixture.

<u>Grate:</u> To rub food, such as hard cheeses, vegetables or whole nutmeg or ginger, across a grating surface to make very fine pieces.

<u>Grease:</u> To coat a utensil, such as a baking pan or skillet, with a thin layer of fat or oil. Use a pastry brush, paper napkin or piece of paper bag to grease pans.

<u>Preheat:</u> To heat an oven to a specific temperature before use.

<u>Sauté:</u> To quickly cook something on both sides in a small amount of oil in a shallow pan, until golden brown.

<u>Toss:</u> To mix ingredients lightly by lifting and dropping them, using two utensils.

BREAKFAST

I always start my morning with breakfast. Sometimes it's traditional like hot cereal or eggs. Most often, it's leftovers! Soup is wonderful on a cold morning, and pasta salad is great when it's hot. We even have Breakfast for Dinner when we need a simple and filling meal at day's end.

BAKED OATMEAL

3 eggs

1/3 cup olive oil

1 teaspoon vanilla

1/2 cup brown sugar

3 cups old fashioned rolled oats

2 teaspoons baking powder

1/2 teaspoon salt

1/2 teaspoon cinnamon

1/2 teaspoon cardamon (optional)

1 cup milk

1 apple or pear, peeled, cored, and chopped

1/4 cup almonds, walnuts, or pecans, chopped

1/4 cup maple syrup or applesauce, plus more for drizzling

Preheat oven to 350 degrees.

In a medium bowl, add the eggs and beat. Then whisk in the olive oil, vanilla, and brown sugar.

In a separate bowl, add the rolled oats, baking powder, salt, cinnamon, (cardamon, if using), and milk. Stir until well mixed. Then add the egg mixture to oat mixture and stir to combine. Transfer into a 9" baking pan.

In another bowl, toss to combine apple (or pear), nuts and maple syrup (or applesauce). Then spread over the oatmeal mixture. Bake for 25-30 minutes until golden brown. To serve, drizzle with maple syrup or applesauce.

Pro Tip: Baked oatmeal can be cut into pieces, frozen and reheated in the oven or microwave.

Serves: 4-6   Prep Time: 15 min.   Cook Time: 30 min.

MUSHROOM AND SCALLION FRITTATA

2 Tablespoons olive oil

12 scallions

1/2-pound brown mushrooms, de-stemmed, caps cleaned, sliced

Salt and pepper, to taste

1/4 teaspoon cayenne pepper

8 large eggs

1/2 cup parmesan cheese, grated

Preheat oven 350 degrees.

Heat the olive oil in a large ovenproof skillet over medium heat. Add the scallions, mushrooms and 1/2 teaspoon salt. Cover; cook, stirring occasionally until the mushrooms are very soft, about 15 minutes. Uncover; cook, stirring until the liquid has evaporated.

Meanwhile, in a medium bowl, whisk together the eggs, cayenne pepper and 1/4 teaspoon each salt and pepper. Pour mixture into skillet.

Using a heatproof spatula, pull back the cooked eggs so that the runny parts go underneath. Cook 4 to 6 minutes. Sprinkle with cheese and transfer to oven. Bake until the center is set, and the top is golden brown, 8 to 10 minutes.

Loosen with spatula and cut into wedges. Serve warm with tomato jam, salsa, sour cream, or chopped parsley.

Makes: 6 cups   Prep Time: 15 min.   Cook Time: 50-60 min.

GRANOLA

3 cups old fashioned rolled oats

1/2 cup toasted wheat germ

1/2 cup sliced almonds

1/3 cup honey

1/3 cup orange juice

1/2 teaspoon ground cinnamon

1 cup flaked coconut

1 handful dried cranberries or raisins

Preheat oven to 325 degrees.

In a large mixing bowl, stir together the oats, wheat germ and almonds.

In a small saucepan, stir together the honey, orange juice and cinnamon. Heat until just boiling, then remove from heat. Add the honey mixture to the oat mixture, tossing gently until coated. Spread oatmeal mixture onto a lightly oiled baking sheet. Bake for 20 to 30 minutes.

Transfer oats to a large bowl. Add coconut and stir. Return to baking pan and bake for an additional 15 to 30 minutes, until lightly browned, tossing once.

Remove from oven and add cranberries or raisins.

Serves: 4   Prep Time: 25 min.   Cook Time: 8-10 min.

FRIED GREEN TOMATOES

4 green tomatoes, sliced into ¼ inch thick

1 cup buttermilk

1/2 cup cornmeal

1/2 cup flour

Salt, pepper

Cayenne pepper to taste

Oil for frying

Sprinkle sliced tomatoes with salt and place on a paper towel or cloth to drain for 20 minutes. Pat dry.

In a medium bowl, add cornmeal, flour, salt, pepper, and cayenne. Mix to incorporate. Pour buttermilk into separate bowl.

Heat oil over medium heat in a frying pan. Dip the tomatoes in the buttermilk, then dredge in the cornmeal/ flour mixture. Fry until golden brown and crispy, about 3 to 4 minutes each side. Drain on paper towels. Serve warm.

Pro Tip: If you don't have buttermilk on hand, add 1 Tablespoon lemon juice or white vinegar to 1 cup whole milk.

Serves: 8-10   Prep Time: 10 min.   Cook Time: 10 min.

MARJORAM HERB BUTTER

8 Tablespoons butter, softened to room temperature

4 Tablespoons fresh marjoram, finely chopped

1/4 teaspoon fresh lemon juice

Salt and pepper, to taste

In a medium bowl, add the butter, marjoram, and lemon juice. Mix to incorporate and season with salt and pepper. Using your hands, roll it into a log on waxed paper. Transfer to freezer for 10 minutes.

Remove from freezer and slice. Serve with fresh baked biscuits. Also try on steamed green beans, broccoli, carrots, zucchini, and corn on the cob.

Serves: 6-8   Prep Time: 5 min.   Cook Time: 5 min.

SPICY CILANTRO CHUTNEY

2 bunches cilantro

1 to 2 jalapeno peppers, seeded and roughly chopped

1/2 teaspoon salt

1 1/2 Tablespoons oil

In a blender, add the cilantro, jalapenos and salt and chop roughly. Gradually add the oil and process until smooth. Serve with scrambled eggs.

Serves: 8-10   Prep Time: 20 min.   Cook Time: 70-85 min.

TOMATO JAM

1 Tablespoon extra-virgin olive oil

2 small cloves garlic, mince

1 one-inch piece ginger, peeled and minced

1 small red onion, peeled and finely diced

4 cups diced tomatoes

1/2 cup red wine, balsamic or rice vinegar

1/4 cup honey

1/4 cup firmly packed brown sugar

1/2 teaspoon ground ginger

Pinch of ground cloves

2 cinnamon sticks

2 whole star anise

In a medium saucepan over medium heat, add the olive oil, garlic, ginger, and red onion. Sauté until translucent about 10 minutes. Then add the tomatoes, vinegar, honey, brown sugar ginger, cloves, cinnamon, and star anise.

Over medium-low heat, simmer, stirring occasionally, until liquid has evaporated, about 60 to 75 minutes. Discard cinnamon sticks and star anise before serving. The jam will keep for 4 days in the refrigerator.

Pro Tip: In the winter, substitute canned tomatoes in water for fresh.

Serves: 10   Prep Time: 15 min.   Cook Time: 3 hrs. (optional)

HERBED CREAM CHEESE

2 8-ounce packages cream cheese, softened

1/2 stick butter (1/4 cup), softened

1 clove garlic, finely minced

1 Tablespoon each fresh herbs of dill, parsley, basil, thyme
 lemon balm, chives

Salt and pepper, to taste

Splash of lemon juice

In a large bowl, mix cream cheese and butter together. Add the garlic and herbs and mix thoroughly. Season mixture to taste with salt and pepper. Then add enough lemon juice to make the cheese smooth.

To use immediately, load a pastry bag with cheese and pipe onto crackers. Top with sliced tomato.

For later use, form into a ball and roll in mixture of herbs, sunflower seeds or ground paprika. Cover and chill in the refrigerator. Serve at room temperature. This is yummy on bagels.

Pro Tip: If you don't have a pastry bag on hand, you can use a sandwich bag with one of the corners snipped off.

SOUP

On an extremely cold day, I visited my husband at work. A bowl of steaming hot soup, which had been cooked over an open fire, was placed in my hands. Chunks of potato, tomato, onion, and garlic jostled for space with the lentils, oregano, and surprisingly, tender neck-bone. The broth was redolent with the herbs and vegetables, and that soup willed me, body, and soul, as no other meal had ever done before or since.

I am always deeply touched by the comfort provided by a humble pot of soup.

Serves: 6-8   Prep Time: 20 min.   Cook Time: 45-50 min.

NECK-BONE SOUP

1 pack of beef neck-bones, approximately 2 pounds

2 onions, chopped

6 cloves of garlic, chopped

1 can of diced tomatoes

half a winter squash, peeled and diced

2 carrots or 1 chayote, peeled and diced

Big pinches of oregano, marjoram, and thyme

1/2 cup rice or 1/4 pound spaghetti noodles

Salt and pepper, not too much of either!

Brown the neck bones in oil, then add the vegetables and cover everything with boiling water. After about 15 minutes, skim the skunge off the top of the soup (what is that stuff anyway?!).

Add the herbs, salt, and pepper, and simmer the soup until the veggies are soft, about 20 minutes. Add rice or noodles and cook an additional 15 minutes.

Fish the neck-bones out of the soup to cool while you ladle the broth and veggies into bowls. Cut the meat off the bones, and don't be picky. Eat the gristle too!

Pro Tip: Follow it up with Fruit Crumble (pg. 71) made from peaches harvested, sliced and frozen during the long August days of summer gone by.

Serves: 4-6   Prep Time: 75 min.   Cook Time: 15-20 min.

WINTER SQUASH SOUP

1 red onion, quartered

2 large apples or pears, quartered

1 head garlic

2 butternut squash

1 large Kabocha squash or pumpkin

1 can coconut milk

2 1/2 cups water or vegetable broth

1 teaspoon ground ginger

1 cinnamon stick

salt and pepper

plain, Greek, or Skyr yogurt

Preheat the oven to 350 degrees.

Place the onion, apples (or pears), garlic, and winter squash on a parchment paper lined baking sheet. Roast for 1 hour. Remove from oven and let sit until cool enough to handle.

Peel the roasted squash and place half in a blender. Squeeze the flesh of the cooled fruit, onion, and garlic into the blender, add 1 cup of water or broth and purée the mixture. Place in stockpot. Purée the rest of the squash with the coconut milk and add it to the pot. Add the ginger and cinnamon stick. Simmer over low heat.

Top each serving with a spoonful of yogurt and toasted pumpkin seeds.

Serves: 4   Prep Time: 20 min.   Cook Time: 30 min.

SWISS CHARD AND LENTIL SOUP

1 cup lentils, rinsed

6 cups water

1 bay leaf

Several sprigs of fresh thyme or 1 teaspoon dried thyme

2 Tablespoons olive oil

1 medium onion, peeled and chopped

1 teaspoon garlic, minced

1 teaspoon ground coriander

1/2 teaspoon cayenne pepper

1-pound Swiss chard, washed and sliced thinly

1 lemon, cut in wedges

Salt and pepper, to taste

In a large soup pot, add the lentils, water, bay leaf and thyme. Bring to a boil. Reduce heat and simmer for 30 minutes, until lentils are tender.

In a skillet over medium heat, warm the olive oil. Add the onion and cook, stirring, until it softens. Add the garlic, coriander, cayenne, and Swiss chard. Cook until Swiss chard wilts, about 5 minutes.

Add the Swiss Chard mixture to the lentils and stir. Season with salt and pepper. Serve with a squeeze of fresh lemon juice in each bowl.

Serves: 6   Prep Time: 10 min.   Cook Time: 20 min.

SPICY TOMATO SOUP

1 large can whole peeled tomatoes

1 whole red onion, chopped

3 cloves garlic

1 bunch cilantro, chopped roughly

4 cups vegetable or chicken broth

1 cup cooked black beans, drained

1 cup cooked corn, drained

1/2 Tablespoon chipotle pepper in adobo

Salt and pepper, to taste

2 avocados, diced

Sour cream or plain Greek yogurt

Low salt tortilla chips

Leftover cooked chicken or shrimp (optional)

Blend the tomatoes, onion, garlic, cilantro, and broth together. Place in soup pot, with black beans, corn, and chipotle pepper. Cook over medium heat for 20 minutes. Add salt and pepper, to taste.

Serve topped with diced avocado, a spoonful of sour cream or yogurt and a handful of crumbled tortilla chips.

Pro Tip: Leftover adobo can be wrapped in wax paper or plastic wrap and frozen for future use. Cooked chicken or shrimp can be added for the last 5-7 minutes for added protein.

Serves: 6   Prep Time: 15 min.   Cook Time: 75 min.

JUMBO TURKEY STEW

1 package smoked turkey legs (3 in a pack)

1 red or yellow onion, peeled and sliced

2 sweet potatoes peeled and diced

3 carrots, cut into chunks

1 large turnip, peeled and diced

2 tomatoes, diced

or 2 Tablespoon sundried tomatoes or 1 can diced tomatoes

5 cloves garlic, minced

1 cup water or apple juice/cider

1 apple, peeled and sliced

1-2 Tablespoon salt and pepper

1 Tablespoon dried marjoram, thyme, and oregano

or 4 sprigs of each herb

1-2 cups water or vegetable broth

1 handful of frozen peas

1 cup precooked rice, barley, or noodles, drained and rinsed

optional: 1 Tablespoon of miso paste (I use brown rice miso)

Preheat oven to 350 degrees.

Plop the turkey legs onto a roasting pan and spread the onion, sweet potatoes, carrots, turnips, tomatoes, garlic, and apple slices around them. Sprinkle with the salt, pepper, and herbs. Pour the water or apple juice into the pan, and bake, covered, for 45 minutes.

Remove the veggies, apples, and any liquid that has accumulated from the pan and put them in a soup pot. Pour enough water or vegetable broth over the veggies to cover them and put the pot on simmer.

Return the turkey legs to the oven, uncovered, for 15-20 minutes. Remove the legs from the oven, cut the meat off them and add them to the soup pot with the rice, barley or noodles, and the peas and miso paste, if using. Simmer, stirring occasionally, for 10 minutes.

Pro Tip: Try this another way! My friend taught me this and it is divine. Perfect to make on a long, chilly day when all ya wanna do is putter around the kitchen.

Simmer a turkey carcass (leftover from a holiday dinner) down in 3 bottles of beer (cheap stuff is ok) and a cup of water, with 2 stalks of mashed, fresh lemongrass stalks, some oregano and parsley, and salt and pepper for 4 hours. Stir every now and then. Add a bag of frozen mixed vegetables and cook for another 15 minutes. Oh, it's SO good!

Serves: 4-6   Prep Time: 15 min. Cook Time: 45 min.

RED LENTIL VEGGIE SOUP

1/2 cup red lentils

3 cups water

1 teaspoons salt

1/2 teaspoon turmeric

1/2 teaspoon cumin seeds, or 1/4-1/2 teaspoon ground

1 Tablespoon ground ginger

1/4 teaspoon cayenne pepper

1/2 red onion, chopped

2 cloves garlic, minced

2 Tablespoon oil or butter

1 sweet potato, peeled and diced

1 cup sliced chayote or zucchini

1 head of cauliflower or

1/2 butternut squash, peeled and cubed

1 chopped tomato

Rinse and drain the lentils and combine with the water in a saucepan. Stir in the salt, turmeric, cayenne and bring to a rolling boil over medium heat. Skim off white foam. Reduce the heat to low, add the sweet potato, chayote (or zucchini) and the cauliflower (or squash). Simmer uncovered for 20 minutes, stirring occasionally.

Meanwhile, heat the oil or butter in a skillet over high heat for 30 seconds.

If using cumin seeds, add the cumin seeds and cook for 1 minute until seeds begin to sizzle and pop. Then add garlic, ginger, onion, and tomato.

If using ground cumin, add to the heated oil the cumin, garlic, ginger, onion, and tomato.

Toss gently for 1 minute. Reduce the heat to medium and cook for 5 minutes, stirring occasionally.

Add the onion mixture to the lentils and continue cooking 5 to 10 minutes, or until the lentils are cooked.

Serve with whole wheat tortillas heated up in a little warm butter.

Serves: 8   Prep Time: 20min.   Cook Time: 75 min.

CHICKEN SOUP WITH CORNMEAL DUMPLINGS

1 whole chicken, cut into pieces, giblets removed (I cook these for my dog)

1 head garlic, cut in half crosswise (no need to peel it)

1 large onion, peeled and chopped

1-2 carrots, chopped

1 large tomato, chopped or 1 can diced tomatoes

1 large sprig fresh oregano, or 1 teaspoon dried oregano

1 large sprig fresh thyme, or 1 teaspoon dried oregano

1 bunch cilantro, chopped

Enough water to cover everything

Salt and pepper to taste

1 cup cornmeal

1 cup flour

1 cup shredded Cojito or Monterey Jack Cheese

Place chicken, garlic, onion, carrots, tomato, oregano, thyme, and cilantro in soup pot, and add enough water to cover everything. Add salt and pepper, to taste. Cook over medium low heat for 45 to 60 minutes, until the chicken is cooked through, stirring occasionally.

In a bowl, mix cornmeal, flour, and cheese. Stir while adding enough of the chicken broth to make a soft dough. Pinch off pieces of dough and drop into simmering soup for 10 minutes.

SALADS AND SIDES

I love salad's versatility. By adding beans, meat or nuts, green salads become a whole meal. When I went on a road trip to promote my work as a culinary educator, people absolutely flipped for this first recipe. I called the journey my Southern Kale Salad Tour. No need to peel the garlic or ginger since they get blitzed in a blender.

Serves: 6   Prep Time: 20 min.   Cook Time: 20 min.

GARLICKY KALE SALAD

3 cloves garlic

1/2 cup lemon juice

1/4 cup soy sauce

3 inches fresh ginger

1/2 teaspoon black pepper

1 cup olive oil

1 bunch kale, washed, stems removed, and chopped small

1 cup red cabbage, thinly sliced

1/2 cup dried cranberries

1 cup canned garbanzo beans

In a blender, add the garlic, lemon juice, soy sauce, ginger and black pepper and purée. Using the lid opening, slowly add olive oil with the motor running on low to thicken the dressing.

In a large bowl, add kale, cabbage, cranberries, and garbanzo beans. Pour dressing into the bowl and toss to coat. Mix thoroughly and let salad sit for at least 20 minutes. This tastes best if it sits for several hours in the fridge.

Serves: 6   Prep Time: 15 min.   Cook Time: 30 min.

BLACK BEAN SALAD

2 cans black beans, rinsed and drained

2 cans corn, rinsed and drained

1 cup cilantro, finely chopped

1 red or orange bell pepper, finely diced

1 small red onion, finely diced

1/2 fresh jalapeno or 1 pickled jalapeno, finely diced

1 cup olive oil

1/4- 1/2 cup apple cider vinegar

Salt and pepper and squeeze of lime to taste

In a large bowl, combine all ingredients and toss. Let chill for at least 30 minutes in the fridge. Serve with tortilla or plantain chips.

Pro Tip: Add cooked shrimp, roasted chicken, or shredded cheese. Or try substituting black eyed peas or navy beans for black beans, basil for cilantro.

Serves: 4   Prep Time: 10 min. Cook Time: 5 min.

RAW SUMMER SQUASH SALAD

2 squash (yellow, zucchini, patty pan or crooked neck),
halved lengthwise and thinly sliced

2 scallions or 1 small red onion thinly sliced

2 teaspoons fresh thyme

1 teaspoon fresh mint, minced

3 Tablespoons fresh lemon juice

3 Tablespoons olive oil

Salt and pepper, to taste

In a medium bowl, whisk together lemon juice, olive oil, salt, and pepper. Add squash, scallion (or onion), thyme, and mint. Toss to incorporate dressing.

Let salad sit for 5 minutes. Serve.

Serves: 4   Prep Time: 20 min.   Cook Time: 20 min.

SHREDDED BEET AND BEET GREEN SALAD

4 raw medium sized red beets (about 1 pound),
peeled and shredded

3 cups beet greens and stems, washed, dried, and sliced

1 1/2 Tablespoons olive oil

1 1/2 Tablespoon balsamic vinegar

1 Tablespoon Dijon mustard

2 cloves fresh garlic, minced

Salt and black pepper, to taste

In a large mixing bowl, toss together the beets and greens.

In a separate bowl, whisk together the olive oil, vinegar, Dijon mustard and minced garlic. Pour the dressing over the salad and toss to coat. Season to taste with salt and pepper.

Allow the salad to stand at room temperature for 15-20 minutes before serving.

Pro Tip: Add some toasted pecans, goat cheese or orange slices to spice it up a bit!

Serves: 4   Prep Time: 10 min.   Cook Time: 5 min.

PEAR AND SPINACH SALAD

1 cup olive oil

1/3 cup rice vinegar

2 teaspoons Dijon mustard

Salt and pepper, to taste

2 pears, cored and sliced

2 apples, cored and sliced

1 large bunch spinach, washed, dried, and chopped

1/4 cup dried cranberries

In a bowl, whisk together olive oil, vinegar, mustard, salt, and pepper.

In a separate bowl, combine pears, apples, spinach, and dried cranberries. Pour the dressing over combined ingredients and toss to incorporate dressing. Serve immediately.

Serves: 4   Prep Time: 5 min.   Cook Time: 30 min.

CUCUMBER DILL SALAD

3 cucumbers, peeled and thinly sliced

1 red onion, peeled and thinly sliced

1/2 teaspoon salt

5 Tablespoons sugar

5 Tablespoons vinegar

1 large sprig fresh dill

In a large bowl, add the cucumbers and red onion. Sprinkle with salt. Cover and refrigerate for 30 minutes.

Remove from refrigerator and drain water from the bowl.

In a small bowl, combine the sugar and vinegar. Pour mixture over chilled cucumbers. Add fresh dill to taste. Serve immediately.

Serves: 6   Prep Time: 20 min.   Cook Time: 10 min.

LETTUCE SALAD WITH HEALTHIER RANCH DRESSING AND CROUTONS

1 head lettuce, torn (about 6 cups)

4 radishes, thinly sliced

For Dressing:

1/2 to 3/4 cup plain yogurt

1 teaspoon dried dill weed

Salt and pepper, to taste

1 clove garlic

2 Tablespoons Parmesan cheese, grated

6 Tablespoons olive oil

For Croutons:

2 cups French bread, sliced

1 Tablespoon olive oil

Large pinch dried oregano

Large pinch dried thyme

1 shake cayenne pepper

For the Croutons: Preheat oven to 400 degrees. Mix olive oil and herbs together, and brush onto bread slices. Bake for 7-9 minutes, until golden, turning once. Break into pieces when cool.

For the Dressing: In a blender, add yogurt, garlic, Parmesan, dill weed, salt and pepper and blend until smooth. Using the lid opening, slowly add olive oil with the motor running on low to thicken the dressing. Use immediately or will store up to 1 week in the fridge.

Combine salad ingredients, dressing and croutons. Serve immediately.

Serves: 4 Prep Time: 20 min. Cook Time: 2 hrs.

HERBED CHICKEN SALAD

1/2 cup parsley

1/2 cup scallions, roughly chopped

3 Tablespoon rice vinegar

1 Tablespoon whole grain mustard

1 teaspoon honey

1/2 cup plain yogurt

2 teaspoons fresh thyme

2 teaspoons olive oil

1/2 teaspoon salt 1 clove garlic

1 1/2 cups cooked chicken breast, chopped

3/4 cup celery, chopped

1 cup cherry tomatoes, cut in half

2 Tablespoons sliced almonds

In a blender, combine the parsley, scallions, rice vinegar, mustard, honey, yogurt, thyme, olive oil, salt, and garlic. Blend until smooth.

In a bowl, combine parsley mixture, chicken, celery, tomatoes, and sliced almonds. Stir until ingredients are well incorporated. Chill at least 2 hours.

Serve with salad greens.

Serves: 4   Prep Time: 20 min.   Cook Time: 20 min.

ROASTED PEPPERS WITH FETA AND MINT

1-pound small, sweet bell peppers

3 Tablespoons olive oil

Salt, to taste

1/4 teaspoon red pepper flakes

1/4 cup fresh mint, chopped

Juice of half a lemon

1/4 cup crumbled feta cheese

Preheat broiler to high.

In a large bowl, add the bell peppers, 2 Tablespoons olive oil, salt, and red pepper flakes. Stir to coat.

Place bell peppers in a single layer on a baking sheet. Broil peppers, turning frequently, until blistered, for about 10 minutes. If you don't have a broiler, peppers can also be grilled over the burner flame, turning frequently with tongs. Place the roasted peppers in a paper bag or a covered bowl and rest 10 minutes.

Once cooled, remove the loosened, blackened skin and the seeds and discard. Transfer the peppers to a bowl and toss with the remaining Tablespoon of olive oil, mint, lemon juice and feta cheese.

Serve with crackers as an appetizer or with roast lamb as a side dish.

Serves: 4   Prep Time: 5 min.   Cook Time: 5 min.

GINGER CARROT DRESSING

2 medium carrots, peeled and chopped

1 inch piece of fresh ginger, chopped

1/4 cup water

2 Tablespoons toasted sesame seeds

1 Tablespoon soy sauce

2 Tablespoons rice wine vinegar

2 1/2 Tablespoons of honey

2 teaspoons sesame oil

1/2 cup vegetable oil

In a blender, add the carrots and ginger and purée, stopping to scrape down the sides of blender. Once puréed, add the water, sesame seeds, soy sauce, rice wine vinegar, and honey and blend until smooth, about 30 seconds. Using the lid opening, slowly add the sesame and vegetable oils with the motor running on low. Blend until dressing is thick and creamy

Serve on your favorite green salad or with fresh veggies. This is especially yummy on raw spinach.

Serves: 4   Prep Time: 15 min.   Cook Time: 15 min.

BEET GREENS WITH WHITE BEANS AND BACON

4 cups white beans, cooked

Greens from 6 bunches beets, washed, dried, and

cut into strips (about 7 cups)

2 Tablespoons olive oil

3 Tablespoons balsamic vinegar

Salt and pepper

1/2-pound bacon

In a large skillet, cook the bacon until it is crispy. Transfer the bacon to a plate lined with paper towels and drain. Reserve the grease in the skillet. Once cooled, crumble the bacon, and set aside.

Using the same skillet with the reserved bacon grease, add the olive oil and heat over medium-high heat. Add the beet greens, scraping the pan and letting the greens wilt. Reduce the heat to low and cook for 5 minutes. Stir in the vinegar, beans, bacon, salt, and pepper. Toss gently and cook until heated through.

Serves: 4   Prep Time: 15 min.   Cook Time: 20 min.

SESAME GREEN BEANS

1-pound green beans, parboiled, rinsed, and drained

2 Tablespoons olive oil

1 1/2 Tablespoons soy sauce

1 Tablespoon toasted sesame oil

1 clove garlic, minced

1 Tablespoon sesame seeds

In a large skillet, heat the olive oil and garlic over medium heat. Sauté until the garlic is soft but not brown, about 1 minute.

Mix in the green beans and sesame oil. Cook 4 to 5 minutes, stirring frequently, until the beans are bright green and crisp but tender when bitten.

Add the soy sauce and stir frequently for 3 minutes. Add the sesame seeds and remove from the heat. Let sit for 10 minutes before serving.

MAIN COURSE

When Zen was 3 and I was pregnant with Zazu (and tired!), he asked, "What's for dinner, Mommy?" "Leftovers," I replied. Since he'd never had leftovers before (my food is so good, there's never anything left in the pot!), I had to explain what they were. "Uukk, I don't want that," he exclaimed! To which I replied, "Well, that's what there is. Eat it or be hungry."

A bit later, I got a call from my mom who lived three houses over, "Your son is down here." "What?! Zen had left the house without telling me?" Yes, he came here and said, "Gramma, tell mommy to make me some new food." "Send him home." How dare he go and fink to my mother about my culinary plan for the evening! If you doble the recipe of the dishes, you'll have enough for lunch or to freeze for a later dinner.

Serves: 6   Prep Time: 20 min.   Cook Time: 10 min.

BEANS-GREENS TACOS

Vegetable oil, enough to coat corn tortillas

6 corn tortillas

2 cups black or pinto beans, rinsed and drained

1/2-pound collard greens, shredded

1 cup shredded Monterey Jack or Cheddar cheese

2 cups tomatoes, diced

3 scallions, sliced

1/2 bunch cilantro, chopped

1 lime, sliced into wedges

Hot sauce or salsa

Preheat the oven to 400 degrees.

Add the vegetable oil to a large casserole dish. Dip each corn tortilla into the oil and place on a baking sheet. Bake for 10 minutes or until golden brown and crispy.

Meanwhile, in a large pot over medium heat, add the beans stirring occasionally. Cook until warmed.

To plate, layer tortillas with beans, cheese, collards, tomatoes, scallions, and cilantro. Serve with lime, hot sauce or salsa.

Serves: 6-8   Prep Time: 20 min.   Cook Time: 20 min.

RICE AND STUFF

2 Tablespoons olive oil

1 medium onion, sliced thinly

1/2 head cabbage, sliced thinly

4 cloves garlic, minced

3 carrots, shredded

1 medium bell pepper, sliced thinly

4 scallions, sliced lengthwise

1 inch piece fresh ginger root

Pinch of red pepper flakes

2 Tablespoons soy sauce

3 cups cooked rice

In a large skillet heat olive oil over high heat. Add the onions and cook for 5 minutes, stirring frequently.

Then add the cabbage, garlic, carrots, bell pepper, scallions, ginger root, and red pepper flakes. Add the soy sauce and stir. Cover and lower heat to medium. Cook until vegetables are crisp and tender.

Add the cooked rice and stir. Heat thoroughly and serve.

SPICY BLACK BEAN PATTIES

2 Tablespoons olive oil

1 medium onion, thinly sliced

8 cloves garlic, minced

1 teaspoon hot sauce

1 Tablespoon ground cumin

2 cans black beans, drained and rinsed

Salt and pepper to taste

2 large sweet potatoes, boiled or baked, peeled, mashed

2 large eggs, beaten

1 cup plain dried breadcrumbs

Preheat oven to 350 degrees.

Warm 1 Tablespoon of olive oil in a skillet over medium heat. Sauté the onion until soft. Add the garlic, hot sauce, and cumin. Cook until fragrant, about 1 minute.

Remove from heat and transfer to a large bowl. Add the black beans to the bowl and mash with a fork or potato masher, leaving about 1/4 of the bean's whole. Season generously with salt and pepper. Fold in sweet potato, egg, and breadcrumbs.

Brush a baking sheet with the remaining olive oil. Divide black bean mixture into 8 balls of equal size; flatten into patties.

Place patties on the baking sheet an inch apart. Bake 10 minutes. Flip with a metal spatula carefully turn patties and bake 10 more minutes.

Pro-Tip: This recipe can be easily multiplied, and patties frozen for later consumption.

Serves: 6-8   Prep Time: 25 min.   Cook Time: 1.5-2.5 hrs

CHICKEN MEATBALL FRICASSEE

4 carrots, peeled and diced

2 small chickens, cut in pieces

or 8 chicken legs/skinless thighs

2 medium onions, diced

4 cloves garlic, crushed

2 teaspoons salt

3 bay leaves

1 cup ketchup

3 cups water, or enough to cover chicken

Meatball Ingredients

1 1/2 cups rice

Boiling water

2 small zucchini or other summer squash, diced small

1 1/2 pounds ground turkey or beef

2 eggs (optional)

1/2 teaspoon oregano

3 sprigs fresh mint, or 1 teaspoon dried mint

1 teaspoon pepper

1 teaspoon salt

1/4 teaspoon cumin seed

1 small onion, finely chopped

1/2 to 1 cup dry breadcrumbs

Preheat oven to 350 degrees.

In a medium saucepan, cover rice in boiling water and leave to soak for 45 minutes.

In a large bowl, add the squash, meat, rice, eggs, mint, pepper, salt, oregano, cumin seeds, onion, and breadcrumbs. Mix until well incorporated. Using your hands, form meat into balls half the size of an egg.

Place the chicken, meatballs, onion, carrots, garlic, salt, and bay leaves in a Dutch oven.

In a separate bowl, add the ketchup. Whisk in water until dissolved into ketchup. Pour ketchup mixture over the ingredients in the Dutch oven. Bake for 1.5 to 2 hours.

Pro Tip: Meatballs can be cooked immediately or frozen for later. If using the meatballs to serve with spaghetti and tomato sauce, bake at 350 for 20 minutes on an oiled baking sheet. Add to soup or bake and serve with spaghetti and pasta sauce.

Serves: 6   Prep Time: 15 min.   Cook Time: 45 min.

UNSTUFFED SWISS CHARD OR CABBAGE

3 bunches Swiss Chard or 1 head of cabbage, sliced finely

4 cups tomato sauce

1 cup water

Meatballs from Previous Recipe

Place the Swiss chard or cabbage in a large saucepan. Top with the meatballs.

Mix the tomato sauce and water together and pour it over the meatball and Swiss chard or cabbage. Cover tightly and cook over medium heat for approximately 45 minutes.

Serves: 4   Prep Time: 15 min.   Cook Time: 20 min.

GARLIC-CILANTRO FISH

1 bunch cilantro, chopped

4 cloves garlic, chopped

1/2 cup lime juice

Large pinch each salt and pepper

1/4 teaspoon red pepper flakes

4 fish filets of tilapia or red snapper

Preheat oven to 350 degrees.

In a blender, purée cilantro, garlic, lime juice, salt, pepper, and red pepper flakes.

Place fish in skillet or on cookie sheet. Pour cilantro mixture over fish filets. Bake for 20 minutes, or until the fish is no longer translucent and flakes easily.

Serves: 6-8   Prep Time: 20 min.   Cook Time: 60 min.

EGGPLANT STEW

1 pound eggplant (1 large or 2 small), diced

4 small or 2 large, sweet peppers, diced

1 medium onion, chopped

1 to 2 cloves garlic, minced

3 large ripe tomatoes, diced or 2 cans diced tomatoes

1/2 cup fresh Italian basil, chopped

1/4 cup olive oil

1 1/2 cups cooked garbanzo beans

Salt and pepper to taste

In a large skillet, over medium-high, heat the olive oil. Add the eggplant and cook until golden brown. Remove from the skillet and set aside.

Lower the heat to medium low, and cook the peppers, onion, and garlic until they are tender, about 10 minutes.

Return the eggplant to the skillet and add the tomatoes. Cook for 20 to 30 minutes, until the tomatoes reduce to a thick sauce.

Stir in the basil, salt, pepper, and garbanzo beans. Remove from heat and serve over polenta.

Serves: 4   Prep Time: 20 min.   Cook Time: 60 min.

GNOCCHI WITH SWEET POTATOES

3 sweet potatoes

1 red onion, sliced

3 cloves garlic, minced

1/2 cauliflower, broken into small pieces

1/4 cup water

Olive oil

Salt and pepper, to taste

red pepper flakes, to taste

1/2 cup raisins, plumped in hot water

1/2 cup sliced almonds, toasted

1 package gnocchi

1/2-pound bacon (optional)

Preheat oven to 350 degrees.

In an oven proof skillet or roasting pan, add the sweet potatoes, red onion, garlic, cauliflower, and water. Drizzle with olive oil and sprinkle with salt, pepper, and red pepper flakes. Stir to coat.

Cover and roast in oven until vegetables are tender, about 45 minutes. Remove the lid, add the raisins and almonds. Stir and cook another 10 minutes, or until the vegetables are lightly browned.

Meanwhile, in a skillet cook the bacon until crispy, then drain and crumble. Cook the gnocchi according to the package and drain.

To serve combine the gnocchi with the vegetables and bacon. Top with parmesan cheese, if desired.

Serves: 4   Prep Time: 30 min.   Cook Time: 30 min.

TUNA/SALMON BURGERS

2 small cans tuna or 1 large can salmon, drained
1 pound of potatoes, boiled, peeled, and mashed
2 scallions, finely chopped
1/2 cup fresh parsley, finely chopped
1/2 teaspoon dried thyme
1/2 teaspoon cayenne pepper
Salt and pepper, to taste
1 cup breadcrumbs
Lemon slices

Preheat oven to 350 degrees.

In a large bowl, add the fish, mash potatoes, scallions, parsley, thyme, cayenne pepper, salt, and pepper. Mash everything together, tasting the mixture and adjusting the seasonings as needed. Form into patties.

Pour the breadcrumbs onto a plate. Then dip each patty into the breadcrumbs. and place on an oiled cooked sheet. Bake for 15-20 minutes, until golden and crispy. Drain on paper towels.

Squeeze lemon juice over each patty and serve.

Serves: 4   Prep Time: 20 min.   Cook Time: 45 min.

CHICKEN OR VEGETABLE CURRY

3 Tablespoon coriander seeds

2 teaspoons black pepper

6 Tablespoons olive oil

1 teaspoon black mustard seeds

2-inch cinnamon stick (or 1 teaspoon ground)

3 1/2 pounds skinned chicken or 3 pounds mixed vegetables
(cauliflower, carrots, yams, peas, squash)

2 medium sized onions, slicked thin

4 cloves garlic, peeled and cut into slivers or minced

1 teaspoon peeled, finely grated fresh ginger

1/2 cup tomatoes, finely chopped

1/2 teaspoon turmeric

1 teaspoon cayenne pepper

1 1/2 teaspoon salt

1 Tablespoon lemon juice

1 can coconut milk

3 fresh hot green chilies, split in half lengthwise
or canned jalapenos

Set a small, cast-iron skillet over medium high heat for 2-3 minutes. Place the coriander seeds and pepper in it. Stir and roast them for 1 1/2 minutes or until they are lightly browned and emit a roasted aroma. Remove the spices, cool them slightly then grind them with a coffee grinder, spice grinder or mortar and pestle.

Put the oil in a wide pot and set over medium high heat. When hot, add the black mustard seeds and cinnamon stick. As soon as the mustard seeds start to pop, put in the chicken, and brown the meat in batches, if necessary.

Once all the chicken is browned, put the onions and garlic into the same pot and turn heat to medium. Stir and fry until the onions are light brown. Add the ginger and tomatoes. Stir and cook until the tomatoes are soft. Turn heat down.

Add the roasted spice mixture, turmeric, cayenne, salt, and lemon juice. Add the coconut milk and enough water to cover the chicken. Bring to a boil, cover, and simmer for 25 minutes, stirring now and then. Add the green chilis to the pot.

Serve with basmati rice, naan or whole wheat tortillas, and sliced mangos for dessert.

Pro Tip: If you are using skinned breasts, brown them as directed, but add them to the sauce for only the last 15 minutes of cooking time.

If you are using vegetables, parboil them and add them to the sauce for only the last 15 minutes of cooking time.

SPICY TUNA SPAGHETTI WITH TOMATO SAUCE

4 cups tomato sauce

2 1/2 Tablespoons extra virgin olive oil

3 cloves garlic, thinly sliced

1 red onion, thinly sliced

1/2 – 1 teaspoon red pepper flakes

12 ounces spaghetti

1 5-ounce can light tuna packed in water, drained

Salt and pepper, to taste

1/2 cup fresh basil, chopped

Bring a large pot of salted water to a boil.

Heat the oil in a saucepan over medium heat. Add the garlic, onion and red pepper flakes and cook, stirring, until the garlic is golden, about 2 minutes. Increase the heat to medium-high, add tomato sauce and 3/4 teaspoon salt and cook, stirring, until the sauce thickens slightly, about 6 minutes. Remove from heat and cover to keep warm.

Add the pasta to the boiling water and cook as the label directs, drain.

Return the saucepan to medium heat, add the pasta and tuna, and cook, tossing, 1 minute. Season with salt and pepper. Remove from the heat and stir in basil.

Serves: 4   Prep Time: 20 min.   Cook Time: 15 min.

PORK AND LEMONGRASS SAUSAGE

2 pounds ground pork

3 cloves garlic, minced or pressed

1 Tablespoon fresh lemongrass or fresh lemon peel, minced

1 teaspoon red pepper flakes

1 cup fresh cilantro, finely chopped

2 Tablespoons fresh ginger, minced

2 Tablespoons soy or Worcestershire sauce

1/2 to 1 teaspoon salt and pepper

In a medium bowl, combine all the ingredients and knead it together with your hands. Form into 4 patties.

In a skillet, heat olive oil over medium heat. Cook until heated all the way through and golden on the outside.

Pro Tip: Unused sausage can be refrigerated for up to one day.

PERFECT ROAST CHICKEN

1 whole chicken

1/4 cup salt

1/2 cup lemon juice

1 head garlic, peeled and minced

1 Tablespoon thyme

1 Tablespoon oregano

1/2 cup parsley, minced

1 whole lemon

2 Tablespoons olive oil

The Day Before: In a small bowl, mix the salt, lemon juice, garlic, thyme, oregano, and parsley together. Rub the mixture onto the chicken skin and inside the bird. Place chicken into a large mixing bowl and cover in plastic wrap. Refrigerate the chicken overnight.

Preheat oven to 350 degrees.

Prick the lemon with a fork and place it inside the chicken. Then drizzle the olive oil on the chicken. Place the chicken onto a roasting pan draped with aluminum foil. Roast the chicken, covered for 45 minutes. Remove foil and roast the chicken until it is done, about 30 additional minutes.

DESSERTS

7 years ago, I traded two dozen of my
cookies for plants. The lady said,
"these are so good, that they are evil."

NANA JUJU'S COOKIES

1 1/2 cups all-purpose flour

1 teaspoon salt

1/2 teaspoons baking soda

1/2 teaspoons ground cardamon

1 cup unsalted butter, slightly softened

1 1/2 cups packed light brown sugar

2 large eggs

1 teaspoon vanilla extract

3 cups uncooked old-fashioned, rolled oats (not instant)

1/2 cup slivered almonds

1/2 cup white or dark chocolate chips

1/2 cup dried cherries or dried cranberries

Preheat oven to 350 degrees.

Leave the cookie sheets ungreased or cover with parchment paper.

In a medium bowl, whisk together the flour, salt, baking soda and cardamon.

In a separate large bowl, cream the butter and sugar together. Beat in the eggs and vanilla. Add the flour, the rolled oats, the fruit, and chocolate, mixing thoroughly after each addition.

Using a soup spoon, drop the batter onto the cookie sheets and bake 12-15 minutes.

Cool on a wire rack, and then eat em' up!

Serves: 8   Prep Time: 35 min.   Cook Time: 25 min.

FRUIT CRUMBLE

8 apples, peaches, or pears, peeled, cored, and sliced

or 4 cups berries

1/4 cup brown sugar

1 teaspoon cinnamon

1 teaspoon cardamom

For crumble topping

1 cup rolled oats

1/2 cup almonds

1/2 cup brown sugar

1 teaspoon cinnamon

1/4 cup olive oil

Preheat oven to 350 degrees.

In a saucepan combine the fruit, sugar, cinnamon, and cardamom. Cook over low heat until the fruit is soft, about 15 to 20 minutes. Transfer the fruit to a pie pan or oven safe skillet and set aside.

Combine the oats, almonds, brown sugar, and cinnamon in a blender. Pulse the mixture until it is a coarse meal. Slowly add the olive oil and pulse the blender until the oats and nuts come together.

Sprinkle the crumble on to the fruit mixture and bake for 25 minutes, or until golden brown.

Pro Tip: Frozen fruit can be substituted for fresh. The crumble topping recipe can be easily multiplied and frozen, ready for a quick dessert.

Serves: 4   Prep Time: 20 min.   Cook Time: 25 min.

FRUIT SAUCE

3 pounds fruit (plums, peaches, blueberries, etc),
peeled, cored, and chopped

1/2 - 1 cup brown sugar

1 teaspoon cinnamon

1 teaspoon cardamom

1 teaspoon vanilla extract

1/4 cup water

Combine fruit, brown sugar, cinnamon, cardamom, vanilla extract, and water in a medium saucepan. Cook over low heat, stirring occasionally until the fruit is soft, about 25 minutes.

Remove from heat and transfer to a large bowl. Mash the mixture with the back of a spoon for a chunky sauce. If you prefer a smooth sauce, purée the mixture in a blender until you reach the desired consistency.

Serve over ice cream and poundcake.

KIDS + FOOD

I gave Zen, my first born, organic rice cereal mixed with boiled water as his first solid food. I wasn't convinced of its nutritional content, much less its taste appeal. I soon stopped using it, and just smushed up whatever we were eating and give it to him. His face got smeared up in the process, but judging from the color of his poops, most of the food got into his mouth. The jars of prepared baby food never seemed appealing, as I imagined a huge vat of goo stewing somewhere in a huge factory.

I skipped rice cereal completely with Zazu. At his 6-month checkup, I told the pediatrician, "He's been eating guacamole, hummus, refried beans and soup since he was 4 months." My boys didn't have problems with gas or allergies from my breastmilk, so I figured that they would be ok eating the food directly. Now I know that a baby's taste preferences are developed during gestation, influenced by the mother's food choices. I wanted to raise Zazu a vegetarian, since we were eating a mostly meat free diet at that time to manage Valentin's cholesterol and weight. However, Vale gave him a chicken bone to gnaw on ("It's good for his gums!" NO, it isn't!!) and it's been a lost cause ever since. Zazu loves meat and helps Valentin slaughter goats and sheep for our meals. We always have a garden in summer, and both kids get a lot of pleasure harvesting peas, tomatoes, and berries out there in the sunshine.

My boys have been involved in food preparation ever since they were about 2 years old. While shopping, we'd count and do color and shape identification. "We need 6 curved yellow pieces of fruit. Can you find that and put it in this bag for me?" They practiced math skills by using the scale in the produce section, estimating costs and by comparing unit prices of grocery items. During meal preparation, the boys cracked eggs into bows, added flour to bread dough, and stirred pancake batter. I gave them avocados to mash into guacamole, cooked, cooled sweet potatoes to dice for curry, and let them push the buttons on the blender when we made smoothies. As they got older, under my supervision, of course, they stood on a chair and stirred pots of soup, poured hot water to make tea, and cut up raw vegetables with a sharp knife. Cooking also served as a means of teaching spelling, reading and math. Zazu loved noodles, so we would choose a recipe from a cookbook together. I'd dictate the grocery list; he'd sound out and spell the words and practiced his handwriting. For example, "If the recipe said 3/4 cup, and we need to double that, how much flour do we need?" I encourage you to include your children in meal planning, shopping, and cooking. One day they'll be able to cook dinner for you and in the meantime, spills can be cleaned up!

I was an obese kid, at my adult weight at 10 years old. In large part, it was due to my lack of activity since I was a bookworm, but also because my parents overfed me. I now realize that they gave me adult sized servings and praised me when I ate it all. "Look who's in the 'Clean the Plate Club'!" I gave my boys little "meals" all day, since their small stomachs could only hold and digest a limited amount at each feeding. A clever idea is to put bits of food in ice trays to serve to your toddler. The portions are more realistic as to what they can eat.

You can save money while feeding your baby nutritious whole foods, here are a couple of recipes for you. No need to add sugar or salt, let the natural sweetness of the vegetable or fruit come through. Remember, do not feed honey to children under 2 years old.

BABY FOOD

Choose one or two of the following:

2 carrots

1 sweet potato

2 apples

2 peaches

Peel, and cut your chosen ingredients into chunks and simmer in hot water until tender. Drain and puree in blender, or mash well with a fork.

You can make in large batches and freeze individual portions in ice trays. To reheat after freezing, warm over low heat or serve at room temperature. Don't save leftover baby food from meal to meal. Toss out whatever is left and serve a fresh cube or new batch at the next meal.

BUYING FRESH + IN SEASON

This chart below gives you an idea of what to look for when you go shopping, and how to store produce when you get home.

SPRING

Arugula

Asparagus

Beets

Broccoli

Cabbage

Carrots

Chard

Collard Greens

Fennel

Garlic Scapes

Greens, Lettuce, Kale

Herbs

Kohlrabi

Leeks

Morels

Onions

Pea Shoots/Greens

Potatoes, New, Sweet

Radish

Scallions

Sorrel

Spinach

Turnips

Zucchini Blossoms

SUMMER

Apples

Beets

Blueberries

Beans, Butter, Green, Shelling

Cabbage

Carrots

Celery

Chard

Cherries

Collard Greens

Corn

Cucumbers

Eggplant

Grapes

Greens, Lettuce, Kale

Herbs

Kohlrabi

Leeks

Melons

Nectarines

Okra

Onions

Peaches

Peas

Peppers, Chili, Sweet

Potatoes, New, Sweet

SUMMER, CONT.

Radish

Scallions

Sorrel

Spinach

Squash, Yellow, Zucchini

Strawberries

Tomatoes

Turnips

Zucchini Blossoms

AUTUMN

Apples

Arugula

Asian Pear

Beets

Broccoli, Broccoli Raab

Brussel Sprouts

Cabbage

Carrots

Celery, Celery Root

Chard

Collard Greens

Cucumbers

Fennel

Garlic

Grapes

Greens, Lettuce and Kale

Herbs

Kohlrabi

Leeks

Onions

Parsnips

Potato, Russet, Red, Yukon, Sweet

Pumpkin

Radish

Radicchio

Scallions

Sorrel

Spinach

Squash, Acorn, Butternut

Tomatoes

Turnips

WINTER

Apples

Beets

Broccoli Raab

Brussels Sprouts

Cabbage

Carrots

Celery Root

Chard

Collard Greens

Fennel

Greens, Lettuce, Kale

Kohlrabi

Leeks

Onions

Parsnips

Potato, Russet, Red, Yukon, Sweet

Radicchio

Sorrel

Spinach

Squash, Acorn, Butternut

Turnips

PRODUCE: BUYING, STORING, COOKING

APPLES:

Apples should be firm. Find different varieties at farmer's markets. They are high in Fiber and Vitamin C.

Keep apples in the crisper of the refrigerator. They are delicious cooked with butter, cinnamon, cardamom, raisins, and ginger. They can be stewed into apple butter, peeled, slice and dried in the oven; peel and cut into chunks and freeze for later use.

BEANS, FRESH:

Choose brightly colored, firm, unblemished beans. Large lumpy beans are likely to be tough. Beans contain folate, to produce red blood cells, and carotene, which the body uses to generate Vitamin A. They are high in Fiber and a good source of Protein.

Beans cook quickly. They store well in the refrigerator for two to three days. Add to soups and stews.

BEANS, DRIED:

Beans are inexpensive and are high in Fiber, Vitamin B6 for support of the nervous system and have Calcium for stronger bones. Beans can be used in soups, salads, main dishes, desserts, dips, and breads.

Beans can be cooked ahead, frozen in 1 cup serving sizes, then added to soups and stews as they cook.

Easy boiled beans: Soak beans overnight in cold water (or boil the beans for 10 minutes, turn off heat and let beans sit for 1 hour). Drain and rinse the beans. Cover with cold water and add one chopped onion and half a head of garlic. Cook over medium low heat for 45 minutes. Add salt to taste and cook beans until tender.

BEETS:

The skin should be smooth, and the greens should be crisp, if attached. Beets contain Folic Acid necessary for rapid cell division and growth during infancy and pregnancy. Our bodies require Folic Acid to produce healthy blood cells and prevent anemia.

Roasting beets concentrates their sweetness. Simply wash the beets thoroughly, heat the oven to 425 degrees, place them on a baking sheet and bake for 1-1.5 hours. When they are ready to eat, gently squeeze the skins; if they collapse, they are ready! They can be peeled and cut into chunks and cooked slowly in a skillet and brown sugar. Their greens can be cooked or eaten raw. Separate, wash and dry beet greens as soon as you get home.

BLUEBERRIES:

Blueberries should be firm and plump. Check containers thoroughly for smashed, shriveled, or moldy fruit. Blueberries contain Vitamin C, Fiber, and Antioxidants. Antioxidants promote the repair of cells which are damage through normal cell function.

Fresh blueberries are perfect eaten fresh and are a delicious addition to muffins, cereal, and pancakes. They can be frozen and kept for months. I add them directly to raw batter without defrosting them first so that my bread doesn't turn out purple! Toss them in a little flour to keep them from sinking into the batter.

CABBAGE:

Heads of cabbage should be firm with bright, crisp leaves with no moist or soft spots. Keep cabbage in the crisper of the refrigerator and use within 2 to 4 days for best freshness. Cabbage contains Vitamin C (promotes tissue repair and growth), Vitamin E (boosts immunity) and Vitamin K (for healthy bones and blood.)

Discard the outer leaves and wash thoroughly. Cut out the core and thick stalk ends. Cook by adding leaves to salted water for 3-5 minutes. Leaves can be steamed for 5 minutes, or stuffed with rice and vegetables or meat, and rolled and baked in tomato sauce.

CARROTS:

When possible, purchase carrots with greens intact. Check tops of carrots for mold. The roots should be firm, with no small white, hair-like rootlets on them; these are old carrots! Carrots are high in fiber, vitamins, and beta carotene. Beta-carotene converts to Vitamin A, which supports healthy eyes, skin, and immunity.

Carrots are versatile vegetables that can be eaten raw, boiled, steamed, roasted or sauteed and are almost always part of a soup stock or base. The tops, though slightly bitter, can be sauteed with garlic, chopped finely and added to salads or made into pesto

COLLARD GREENS:

Firm stems and leaves, brightly colored, unwilted leaves are signs of a freshly picked bunch. Smaller leaves are more tender and milder. Collards should keep fresh for three to five days in a refrigerator.

Collards can be quickly steamed, dressed with a squeeze of lemon juice and served. While "Southern" style collards are usually cooked with pork, substituting lower fat meat such as smoked turkey, or dried mushrooms or miso paste can add a significant boost to the flavor.

CUCUMBERS:

Cucumbers should be firm, with no soft spots. Avoid waxed cucumbers, which may not have been recently harvested. Cucumbers are high in water, which helps rehydrate the body. They store well for a week in the refrigerator.

EGGPLANT:

Stores usually carry either the larger dark purple eggplant, or the smaller, violet Asian eggplant. Look for firm, shiny smooth skins. The fruit should rebound when pressed gently with your thumb. Avoid wrinkled, soft or large fruits, which tend to be bitter. Eggplant keeps well for one to two days on the counter after purchase.

Eggplants stew down into soft yumminess when cooked slowly. They cook quickly on the grill when brushed with olive oil. Eggplants pair naturally with olives, olive oil, onions, bell pepper, tomatoes, and vinegar.

GARLIC:

Garlic heads should be firm, with no green sprouts growing out of the tops. Store at room temperature.

Garlic burns easily at high heat. To peel garlic, lay a clove on its side, and press it with the side of a knife. The skin will loosen. A garlic press is an extremely useful tool to mince garlic quickly.

You can also roast garlic for use in other recipes. To roast garlic, heat the oven to 375. Remove a thin slice from the top of a whole head (or two) of garlic. Drizzle head with olive oil, wrap the garlic in foil or parchment paper, and bake for 40 minutes until it is soft. Squeeze the roasted cloves into soups, salad dressings or on toasted bread.

HERBS:

Herbs make food taste better and are full of antioxidants, which are great for your health. Their essential oils are most potent when the herbs are fresh; dried herbs still retain flavor but lose it the longer they are stored. The general rule for substituting amounts in recipes is to use one teaspoon of dried herbs for each Tablespoon of fresh herbs.

When using fresh herbs, add them toward the end of the cooking time to maintain their flavor. To help herbs last a few days longer, refrigerate them. Leaves and small stems can be wrapped in damp paper towels. Large bunches with long stems can be placed in a small jar of water. Fresh herbs can be mixed with olive oil or butter and frozen to be directly to soups and stews, or thawed, spread on bread, and toasted.

KALE:

Kale should be a deep green color, with crisp leaves. It has a sweet flavor, and chewy texture.

The middle rib is slower to cook than the leaves, and so can be removed and cooked separately. It goes well with bacon, raisins, onions, and garlic. The whole leaf can be eaten raw, and becomes tender with long, slow cooking. Kale has the highest iron content of all leafy greens, so the broth they are simmered in can be saved and added to rice or grains for added nutrition.

MUSHROOMS:

Fresh, moist stems and unbruised, firm caps are the best. Clean the caps gently with a soft brush just before using them. They get soggy if washed: therefore, wipe them off gently with a dry cloth.

Mushrooms are delicious when sauteed over high heat. A lot of water will be released, so keep cooking until the water evaporates and they turn brown. They are great in long, slow braises of meat and vegetables.

OKRA:

Select small pods, between 2 to 3 inches in length. Larger pods tend to be tough. Containers of okra will keep in the refrigerator for 2 to 3 days.

Frying okra quickly in oil prevents the "slimy" texture that makes people avoid this vegetable. Okra is made even more tasty by adding it to garlic, onions, tomatoes, and sweet peppers, cumin, or lemon juice.

ONION:

Mature onions should be hard, with dry skins and no signs of mold. Freshly picked green, or spring onions have firm, green stalks and firm, small bulbs. Onions are considered helpful in lowering blood cholesterol levels. Mature onions may keep in dry storage for 2 to 3 months, while green onions last up to a month in the refrigerator.

Onions are a versatile addition to the cooking pot, since they can be baked, broiled, boiled, roasted, fried, grilled, sauteed or eaten raw. When cooked gently over low heat, the sugar in the onions caramelizes, adding depth to the flavors of the dish. To reduce your tears when cutting an onion, cut the root end off first.

PEACHES:

Tree ripened peaches are treasures of the summer season. Fragrant and juicy, the skins of ripe peaches have a rosy blush and a slight "give" when pressed on the stem end. Avoid peaches that are green and hard; they will not ripen further and are sour. Store peaches on the counter out of direct sunlight. They freeze well when sliced and bagged.

Nothing beats the taste of a ripe peach, warmed by the sun. Blackberries, blueberries, raspberries, and plums make excellent partners in both simple desserts, such as parfait, or in more elaborate pastries such as a tart. Peaches are a surprising addition to salads.

PEARS:

Choose pears with skin that is free of cuts and scratches. Pears don't ripen on the tree, so they may be brought green and left out on a countertop until they yield to gentle pressure.

Softer varieties of pears are best for baking, while firmer varieties are more suited for canning and poaching. Almonds, chocolate, cinnamon, ginger, and honey complement pear's sweet taste.

PEPPERS:

Brightly colored, firm, and shiny peppers are the best choice for sweet peppers. They will keep for a week in the refrigerator. Peppers are high in fiber, Vitamin C and antioxidants which is thought to protect the body from cancer.

Ripe, raw peppers are sweet and crunchy. Peppers' tops can be cut off, the seeds removed, and the cavity filled with a grain or grain/meat mixture and baked in a tomato sauce.

RADISH:

Fresh leaves and firm roots are signs of a ripe radish. They are best used soon after purchase. They contain Vitamin C, and are good with spicy meats, smoked salmon, and sushi.

Radish can be eaten raw, stir-fried, baked, or boiled. They lose their peppery taste when cooked but add texture to stews and soups. The fresh green leaves can be pureed with chopped garlic, lemon, olive oil, and Parmesan cheese to make pesto.

STRAWBERRIES

Berries should be firm and juicy. Check for moldiness in the basket. They are best eaten soon after purchase, although they can easily be spread on a baking sheet, frozen, then bagged. Berries are high in antioxidants and contain Vitamin C. Their taste is complemented by vanilla, lemon, and chocolate.

Sweet, fresh berries make lovely toppings for pound cake, cereal or dropped into seltzer water. Make a simple syrup for flavoring drinks or iced teas by putting equal parts berries, water, and sugar in a saucepan. Cook over low heat for 20 minutes. Clean straw- and blackberries by swirling them whole with stems attached in a bowl of cool water. The grit will fall to the bottom, so, lift them out. Raspberries are very delicate and should be gently brushed clean.

SQUASH:

Squash can be divided into two types: Summer and Winter. Summer squash has edible skin and a mild, slightly sweet flavor. Smaller sized squash tends to be sweeter and less watery than the larger ones. They will last for up to a week. Squash blossoms can also be eaten, and are yummy stuffed with cheese, dipped in a batter and fried.

Winter squash will keep at room temperature for 2 to 3 months. Choose fruits with firm flesh, and a dried stem attached. To peel a butternut squash more easily, cut a thin slice off the bottom of the squash to make a flat surface. Place the squash on a cutting board, hold the squash at the top, and use a sharp knife to slice the skin off.

SWEET POTATOES:

Roots should be heavy, firm, and unblemished. Store them at room temperature and use within a few days of purchase. Sweet potatoes are high in fiber and Vitamin C. Their Vitamin B6 content has a beneficial effect on easing premenstrual syndrome and mild depression.

Sweet potatoes turn brown when peeled, so cover peeled roots with water immediately or cook them whole and unpeeled. They are a delicious addition to bean stews and can be used pureed in bean patties or biscuits.

SWISS CHARD:

The leaves of the chard should be crisp and glossy, with firm stems whose ends appear freshly cut, not dry and shriveled. Chard is high in iron, folic acid and Vitamin C.

The leaf can be cooked whole, or the stems may be removed and served separately. Chopped and added to soups, they add hearty texture to a meal. The leaves can be steamed, stir fried, or used as wraps for grains, meats, and nuts. As with collards, a squeeze of lemon juice or vinegar in the cooking liquid makes their iron content more available for use by your body.

TOMATOES:

Vine-ripened tomatoes are worth waiting for. Juicy and firm, they are full of flavor, perfect with only a sprinkle of salt and pepper. Store at room temperature stem side down, not in the fridge.

Tomatoes can be peeled by pouring boiling water over them in a bowl and letting them sit for 1 minute. Drain and peel them immediately. Use a sharp paring knife to cut just through the skin and the peel will come off easily.

Tomatoes can be stewed, sauteed, roasted or grilled whole. They can be made into sauce and canned or frozen for later use.

TURNIPS:

Choose turnips that are firm and bright. Wrinkled, soft vegetables are old. Store turnips in a cool, dry, and dark space, or in the refrigerator. Young turnips can be thinly sliced and eaten raw or pickled. Larger ones can be roasted, boiled, braised, or pan-fried. The tops are high in Vitamin C and K, which aid in blood clotting.

Turnips are sweet and tender when they are roasted or braised, and make a lovely, filling addition to stews.

PAIRING HERBS + VEGETABLES

VEGETABLE	HERB/SPICE
Artichoke	Parsley, Bay Leaves, Coriander, Paprika
Asparagus	Dill, Marjoram, Nutmeg, Rosemary
Beetroot	Pepper, Coriander, Thyme, Dill, Chives, Ginger, Cloves, Sage
Broccoli	Garlic, Marjoram, Nutmeg
Cabbage	Bay Leaves, Garlic, Curry, Marjoram, Nutmeg, Chives, Parsley
Carrots	Parsley, Basil, Curry, Chives, Sage, Thyme
Cauliflower	Basil, Dill, Mace, Ginger, Curry, Nutmeg, Oregano, Coriander, Mint
Cucumber	Rosemary, Dill, Mustard, Pepper Basil, Chives
Eggplant	Garlic, Parsley, Mint, Sage, Curry, Basil, Rosemary, Oregano
Green Beans	Garlic, Basil, Dill, Nutmeg, Pepper
Leeks	Mustard, Parsley, Dill, Bay Leaves, Thyme, Paprika, Celery Salt
Lettuce	Basil, Chives, Thyme, Tarragon, Dill, Parsley
Mushrooms	Olives, Ginger, Cumin, Parsley, Thyme
Onions	Paprika, Celery Salt, Pepper, Coriander, Basil, Garlic, Marjoram, Sage
Peas	Tarragon, Mint, Parsley, Nutmeg, Sage, Marjoram, Basil
Potatoes	Garlic, Nutmeg, Paprika, Pepper, Rosemary, Thyme
Tomatoes	Basil, Tarragon, Garlic, Chives, Dill, Mint, Oregano, Paprika, Fennel, Parsley, Thyme, Cilantro
Zucchini	Garlic, Basil, Parsley, Oregano

CONSUMER CONSIDERATIONS

For me, eating on a budget involves thinking about several factors:

- Cost

- Pesticide Residue

- Who is growing the food?

- Livestock rearing practices

Space constraints prevent me from growing everything needed to feed my family. I would prefer to purchase only organic produce, but for the most part, its cost prohibits this. I often refer to the Environmental Working Group's annual list of produce with the most and least pesticide residues, The Dirty Dozen and Clean Fifteen. For example, strawberries are usually on The Dirty Dozen, so I grow strawberries at home and purchase them from local organic growers at Farmers' Markets. However, when I had the 7 kids, I had to consider price vs quality. I gave them commercially grown apples, which sold for $2/bag as opposed to organic ones for $2 each.

As I became more interested in the food system, the ethics of the industry became more important to me. How does my consumption of the food impact the lives of those harvesting it and the animals raised as meat? Most of us have the idea that our food is grown by "Ma and Pa" somewhere on a small farm. The reality is that the majority of the food grown in the United States is produced on huge corporate owned farms by migrant farm workers. Grueling labor, low pay, no access to health insurance or even decent living conditions are, unfortunately, the norm. Women often face harassment from their co-workers or farm owners, and there is no recourse for health problems caused by pesticide and herbicide exposure. Stress injuries from repetitive movements are common, and those working in animal husbandry face particular risks. Large volumes of liquid manure are stored below grated floors or outside the sheds in "manure lagoons." Many workers have been instantaneously asphyxiated by the release of hydrogen sulfide gas. Once unconscious, workers quickly drown in the liquid manure.

I recommend the documentaries Rape in the Fields and Food Chains for an eye-opening insight into this part of the American agricultural system.

SELF CARE AS FAMILY CARE

Why is there even a section on self-care in a cookbook? Well, I know from experience, that if I am in good shape-- mentally, emotionally, physically, and spiritually, I can take care of my greatest love and responsibility, my family. I was diagnosed with post-partum depression when Zen was 18 months old. It was due, in part, to the stress of my husband's adjustment to this country, and partly due to exhaustion from mothering my baby. I was nursing my son on request every few hours, and not eating enough food to meet the demands of both his and my own nutritional needs. I struggled to get organized in my mind to plan activities for the day, and by 2pm, I was exhausted and had to take a nap. I was moody, weepy, irritated with my husband, had no interest in sex (ugh! Yet ANOTHER chore to do!), I was ill-kempt and rarely got dressed, the house was a mess. Add to that, I was lonely, paralyzed, and isolated by depression and stress.

Librado, Valentin's oldest son came to live with us when Zen was 18 months old, and in 2003, Zazu was born after I'd had two miscarriages. I'd always planned to have Valentin's other children live with us, so in February 2004, 3 more kids moved in. And THEN, that Mother's Day, my 15-year-old nephew joined the tribe. So, there I was, with 7 kids between 8 months and 20 years old. Since Vale worked 6 days a week, I was the primary child caretaker. My step kids had been neglected and were malnourished, so many hours were spent taking them to the pediatrician, the hearing specialist, various clinics, and special education meetings. I was absolutely worn out. My heart always felt like it was beating weirdly, I was so stressed that I couldn't catch my breath, no matter how much I slept, ate, or hydrated, I never felt rested. Basically, my adrenals were depleted from always being "on". I finally blew a gasket and "ran away" with my little ones to a girlfriend's house in New Mexico for 10 days. Upon my return, I designated Sundays as "Ask Popi Day". Unless you are on fire or have been decapitated, don't ask me for anything." Zazu was the exception since he was still breastfeeding.

Two years later, I was in worse shape. I was always screaming and crying from frustration and exhaustion. However, I was determined to raise the kids, because, after all, I'd brought them here to improve their lives, right?! I couldn't give up on them, could I? I asked a friend "How do you know when you've done enough?" She gave me THE BEST advice that I've ever gotten in my life. She said, "if what you are doing is damaging your health or your relationship with people you are about, it's time to stop." Yes, I was stressed out ALL THE TIME. Despite wanting to care for the kids, I'd become both a lousy mother and stepmother. That summer the kids went to see their mom, and I decided that I couldn't raise them any longer. Their mom was alive. Who would raise my kids if I dropped dead from stress?!

Those two periods of my life, taxing and painful as they were, are ones that I honor. They taught me that, despite my good intensions to care for the children, sacrificing my own health, physical and mental, was helpful to NO ONE. Not my children, not my husband, and definitely not for me. Too often we give and give and give until we are empty, thinking that we aren't good parents, good adult children, good friends, or good partners if we don't give EVERYTHING to another. So many times, I thought "If I give up, I'm not a good person". I had to teach myself that taking time for self-care wasn't a selfish act; it was an act of Self Love. Now, if I am in a stressful situation, I ask myself the two important questions: "is this damaging my health? Is this damaging my relationship with anyone?" If so, I stop what I am doing, and redirect myself. The old saying "If Mama isn't happy, then no-one is happy" is true! I've also taught my children that they need to take care of me, and hopefully, I am modeling the importance of self-care.

ADDENDUM

"The simplest life, like the simplest meal, is cause for celebration."

This is from the essay, A Bowl of Comfort: Simple White Rice by Edwidge Danticat. In it, she describes how her dying father requested and ate a bowl of plain rice. He insisted on sharing it with her and it turned out to be his last meal.

I encourage you to take time to revel in the gift of food. Get so connected with food and its preparation that you fall in love with it. If you have time to stop in the middle of the sidewalk to check your phone, you can take time to make your meals healthy and beautiful.

Tap into your senses as you cook:

Vision: Cook with a rainbow of produce, use a pretty bowl or tablecloth, make a centerpiece of flowers, a leafy branch or produce so that you have something lovely to look at as you dine.

Hearing: Put on your favorite music and dance, listen to the sound of soup bubbling or the rhythmic noise you make as you grate carrots.

Taste: Try an ingredient and enjoy it for its own sake. Imagine how it adds to the whole dish. I don't suggest doing this with raw onions!! Nothing tastes as sublime as a fully ripe tomato or peach.

Touch: What textures do you feel? Are the leaves of the salad greens ruffled or smooth? Is the lemon hard of soft? Savor the motion of mashing potatoes.

Smell: What do the ingredients smell like? Fresh herbs are so very fragrant. Is this milk spoiled? If it is, you can't drink it, but you can use it to make cornbread!

Spirit and Soul: What am I feeling as I'm cooking? What kind of energy am I putting into this meal? Will I or my family or guests be able to taste love in this dish?

You don't have to have a bundle of money to create or offer something beautiful and nourishing to eat. After the birth of my second son, my friend brought me black beans and rice for a postpartum meal. The way that the food was laid out in the container showed me that she'd prepared it with love and intention, and that made it one of the best meals I've ever had.

ABOUT JUJU

If I were a vegetable or fruit, I'd be a tomato because I like to "live juicy", that is, I love to soak up the sun and most folks are happy to see me because I bring a good "flavor" to the scene. Or perhaps I'd be a Calabaza squash since orange is my favorite color. Or Kale because I have a "crunchy" vibe. Summer is definitely my favorite season for produce due to the abundance of it and yum, peaches, THE best food in the world. I firmly believe that healthy food can be easily and inexpensively prepared.

Affectionately known as "Nana" JuJu to my friends creating delicious, nutritious meals with few ingredients is my specialty. I live with my family, including 4 dogs and 7 cats in Maryland, but my heart remains in California, my home state.